Nanuet Public Library
149 Church Street
Nanuet, NY 10954

W9-BCY-086

POOP IS POWER!

Robin Koontz

Educational Media

rourkeeducationalmedia.com

Scan for Related Titles and Teacher Resources

Before Reading:

Building Academic Vocabulary and Background Knowledge

Before reading a book, it is important to tap into what your child or students already know about the topic. This will help them develop their vocabulary, increase their reading comprehension, and make connections across the curriculum.

1. *Look at the cover of the book. What will this book be about?*
2. *What do you already know about the topic?*
3. *Let's study the Table of Contents. What will you learn about in the book's chapters?*
4. *What would you like to learn about this topic? Do you think you might learn about it from this book? Why or why not?*
5. *Use a reading journal to write about your knowledge of this topic. Record what you already know about the topic and what you hope to learn about the topic.*
6. *Read the book.*
7. *In your reading journal, record what you learned about the topic and your response to the book.*
8. *After reading the book complete the activities below.*

Content Area Vocabulary
Read the list. What do these words mean?

anaerobic
bioenergy
biogas
biomass
bioreactor
carbon-neutral
gasifier
methane
microorganisms
nitrates
pathogens
prototype
renewable
sustainable

After Reading:

Comprehension and Extension Activity

After reading the book, work on the following questions with your child or students in order to check their level of reading comprehension and content mastery.

1. *How is converting waste into energy helpful around the world?* (Summarize)
2. *Explain the process for turning waste into energy.* (Infer)
3. *What other readily available materials might be used to create energy?* (Asking questions)
4. *What do you think about cooking with dung?* (Text to self connection)
5. *What other ways can human and animal waste be used?* (Asking questions)

Extension Activity

Be an inventor! Design a toilet that can provide power to your school. What materials would you use? How would the power be generated?

Table of Contents

The Power of Poop!..4

Building a Better Toilet 10

Powerful Poopers...20

Building a Better Poop Digester.........................29

Pros and Cons of Poop Power...........................40

Glossary 46

Index 47

Show What You Know......................................47

Websites to Visit..47

About the Author...48

THE POWER OF POOP!

Walking into a stinky bathroom usually brings up one thought: pee-yew! But Leroy Mwasaru gave that nasty stench more positive thought than most people. Leroy attended Maseno School in Kenya, Africa. When the school expanded its dormitory space to hold more than 700 students, there were problems. The pit-style latrines and primitive sewage system caused the area to smell awful. Plus the massive waste the system produced was polluting local freshwater resources.

Meanwhile, the only cooking fuel at the school was firewood, and the smoke that accumulated inside was choking everyone in the building. So Leroy and his friends figured out a way to solve both of these problems: they would turn their poop into a clean cooking fuel!

The average person produces about 700 pounds (317.51 kilograms) of poop per year.

The students set to work designing a Human Waste **Bioreactor** (HWB). Their contraption would make use of all the latrine sewage along with organic scraps from the kitchen. The waste would be channeled into an underground chamber. Working sort of like a compost heap, **microorganisms** would digest and break down the muck, and in the process, release **biogas**. That gas, which was mostly **methane**, was contained in a tank. Similar to natural gas, it could be used for cooking and heating.

Leroy and his buddies refined their idea with help from other students. Within the year, they had a working system in place with new ideas to improve it.

Leroy hopes to start up his own company someday, with the goal of providing communities like his with clean fuel and healthy sanitation.

A Biogas Reactor

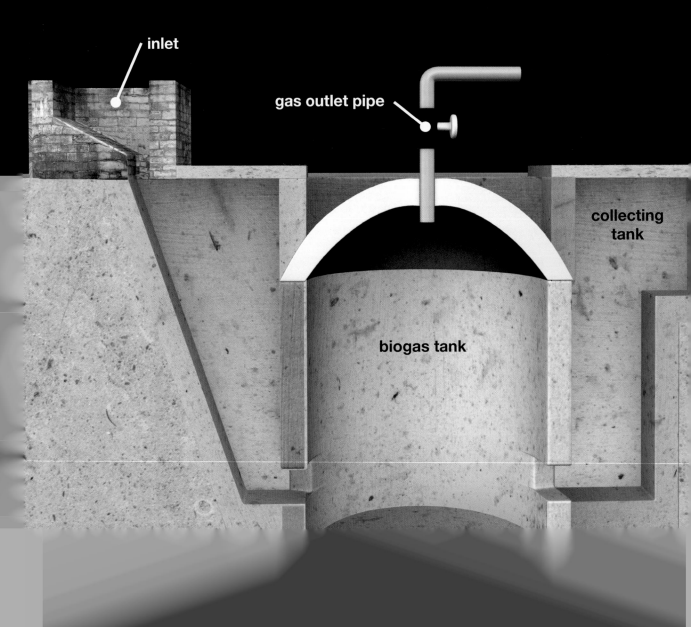

inlet

gas outlet pipe

collecting tank

biogas tank

In many rural areas around the world, wood for cooking fuel can be scarce. Plus, wood fires can cause respiratory problems and other health risks from smoke inhalation. A system similar to Leroy's is being constructed in areas such as Nepal, in South-Central Asia. Single-family biogas plants, or factories, work to collect animal manure, human waste, and plant materials. The

methane gas the plant produces is stored in a gas tank, and a metal pipe with a valve supplies the family with flames for cooking their meals.

Natural Gas

Natural gas is a fossil fuel that was created by the breakdown of organic materials from plants and animals that were alive millions of years ago. The gas is stored beneath Earth's surface.

In India, and many other countries, the hara stove is widely used in rural areas where wood is scarce. The pot used for cooking food sits directly on the dung cakes.

Making use of poop is nothing new despite the pee-yew factor. People have burned dried manure for as long as they've had agriculture and domestic animals. Archaeologists have found ancient evidence of dried dung used as fire fuel in Incan remains. They think the dung fire was used for heat and to cure ceramic pottery.

Early Americans also used dried dung for both heating and cooking. And in modern Egypt, residents use dry animal dung mixed with plant residues. Dung cakes, known as gella or jilla, still make up much of the available cooking and heating fuel in many rural areas.

Poop is just one of the many biological materials, called **biomass**, which has the potential to

create **bioenergy**.

Burning wood is the oldest kind of biomass energy used on Earth. Poop is considered a biogas product because it produces gas. Biogas can also be produced from crops such as corn, wheat, and sugarcane, as well as agricultural waste products and algae. The composting process of all biogas material produces the gas that can potentially help power the world and have a positive impact on climate change. But just how much power is in poop?

Cooking with Dung in the 1880s in America

"Here is the rundown of the operations that mother went through when making baking powder biscuits. ... Stoke the stove, get out the flour sack, stoke the stove, wash your hands, mix the biscuit dough, stoke the stove, wash your hands, cut out the biscuits with the top of a baking powder can, stoke the stove, wash your hands, put the pan of biscuits in the oven, keep on stoking the stove until the biscuits are done (not forgetting to wash the hands before taking up the biscuits)."
— From Western Story: The Recollections of Charley O'Kieffe, 1884–1898. University of Nebraska Press, 1960.

BUILDING A BETTER TOILET

The power that people can gain from what we deposit in our toilets has only recently been explored in innovative new ways—via the toilets themselves. Composting toilets, which basically turn waste into fertilizer, have been around for a long time. Harvesting the sludge from sewer plants and turning the goo into fertilizer is pretty common among many nations in the world.

Humans produce a lot of waste, not only the stuff that goes in the toilet, but all kinds of garbage. Garbage landfills are the third-largest human-related methane producers. The biogas even has its own name, LFG, for landfill gas. The buried debris creates its own **anaerobic** digester. But the good news is that LFG can be captured and used as an energy source.

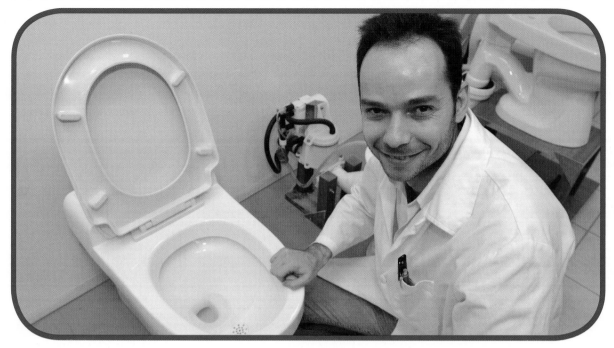

The No-Mix Vacuum Toilet uses vacuum suction technology, just like those used in aircraft lavatories.

The challenge of using that same resource to produce energy cleanly and efficiently has prompted engineers and researchers to come up with new ideas to make good use of poop. They thought toilets were a good place to start.

At the Nanyang Technological University in Singapore, scientists invented a power-producing commode called the No-Mix Vacuum Toilet. The new design uses very little water to flush liquids as well as solids, which is great news for saving water. But this toilet also has the potential to use the waste to generate energy. The resources are completely recovered for use as both power and fertilizer. What goes down comes back around!

The original toilet was called a water closet. The first flushing toilet ever made is believed to be more than 2,800 years old. It was owned by King Minos, of Crete, an island in Greece. The king's "throne" was found in the rubble of his palace many centuries later.

The toilet is already designed to separate the liquids from the solids. The liquid waste gets diverted to a processing facility to be used as fertilizers, including potassium, nitrogen, and phosphorus, which are the main ingredients in commercially sold fertilizers.

The solid waste goes to a bioreactor, where microscopic organisms get to work on it. They munch and digest the gunk, producing biogas. That gas can be used for cooking, gas light and heat, and can also be converted into electricity and/or stored in fuel cells. The process is called anaerobic digestion.

A anaerobic bioreactor operates by adding moisture to the waste. This method of decomposition produces excess amounts of methane which can be recovered through a methane extraction system to generate energy and reduce greenhouse gases.

bioreactor

In 2011, The Bill & Melinda Gates Foundation sponsored the "Reinvent the Toilet Challenge" in an effort to bring waste disposal solutions to the approximately 40 percent of the world's population that doesn't have safe or affordable sanitation available.

Seattle is home to the headquarters of the Gates Foundation, and is the center for their work in global health, global development, and global policy & advocacy.

**Bill Gates
(1955-   )**

RTTC grants were awarded to researchers and engineers who were trying new approaches to create a toilet that could safely manage waste and also make use of it. The rules were that the design had to accomplish several goals while costing less than five cents per user per day. Connections to sewer, electricity, or water were not allowed. The toilet had to remove germs and recover resources such as nutrients, clean water, and energy. It would have to be profitable and **sustainable** enough to encourage investments from sanitation companies. And it would have to be so cool, everyone would want one!

The Gates Foundation gave one of the grants to researchers from RTI International in North Carolina. Their toilet design would convert the waste into burnable fuel, stored energy, and usable water! Begun in 2012, the team planned to work with researchers at the National Aeronautics and Space Administration (NASA) to share ideas about dealing with issues of limited energy and water when dealing with human waste.

Unsafe methods to capture and treat human waste result in serious health problems and death. Food and water tainted with fecal matter result in 1.5 million child deaths every year.

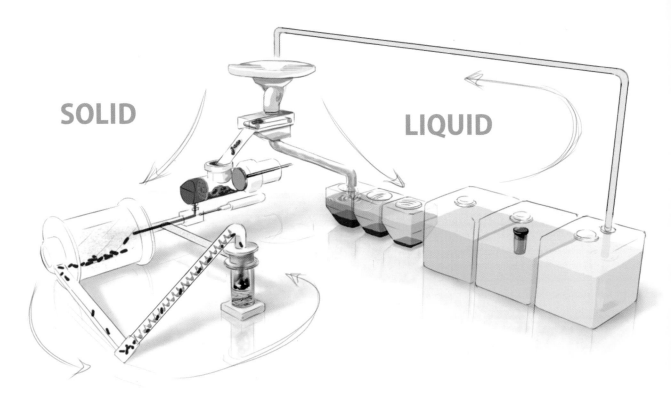

SOLID

LIQUID

The solid waste would be dried once it was separated from the liquids. Solar energy and thermal energy along with natural drafts would cause the drying waste to break down into pellets. The pellets would be burned in another invention, the Thermoelectric Enhanced Cookstove, which was also developed by RTI.

The cookstove would capture some of the heat and convert it into electricity. The electricity would be stored in a battery and later used to power the water treatment processes. That treatment, powered by the poop, would result in disinfected water that would be okay to use as rinse water in the toilet and as fertilizer.

When it was finally done, their toilet would be a self-sustaining waste treatment system. By February 2015, the new design was in the **prototype** phase, with an end goal of creating a toilet that would affordably help create better sanitary environments.

Who knew flushing a toilet could be so productive?

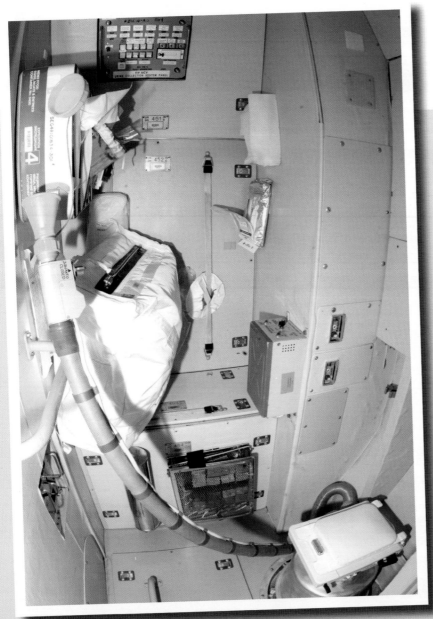

Space Poop

Taking care of human waste while astronauts are in space has been a challenge since the first manned mission. Some researchers are now figuring out ways to use the space poop to line the walls of spacecraft. The stuff would behave like a radiation shield, warding off harmful cosmic rays. Other researchers are working on turning all the waste into rocket fuel. Now that's some powerful poop!

Eat It!

In 2015, NASA funded a project that would attempt to figure out how to recycle human poop into synthetic food. This gunk would become dinner for astronauts during long journeys, or while living on a space colony on Mars. "Technology drives exploration, and investments in these technologies and technologists is essential to ensure NASA and the nation have the capabilities necessary to meet the challenges we will face as we journey to Mars," said Steve Jurczyk, associate administrator for NASA's Space Technology Mission Directorate.

Activity

Design a Toilet!

After reading about the ideas other students and engineers designed to make bioenergy through a toilet design, see what you can come up with. Draw a diagram showing how it would work. Support your design with the science of biogas creation.

According to a recent estimate, a single person's one-day waste output could generate all the electricity needed to keep a 60-watt light bulb lit for nine hours.

POWERFUL POOPERS

Harmful algal blooms are a major environmental problem in all 50 states. Known as red tides, blue-green algae or cyanobacteria, algal blooms have severe impacts on human health, aquatic ecosystems, and the economy.

Animals also create a lot of poop, and they normally don't use toilets. In a natural setting, animal waste slowly breaks down, sometimes is eaten, and overall doesn't have a negative impact on the planet. But the human practice of raising large populations of livestock for meat, milk, and clothing has had a serious influence on the amount of greenhouse gases that are emitted into our atmosphere. All that manure can also put **nitrates** into the groundwater, which can cause blooming algae to form in streams and rivers, which in turn suffocates fish.

What can we do with all of that poop? It can be put to use, just as people have been doing with toilet and sewage waste. When animal manure is enclosed in an anaerobic digester, also called a bio-digester, the composting process speeds up and methane gas is captured. The problem is that there is a whole lot of poop to deal with, and setting up a biogas system to handle it all can be very expensive. Scientists and researchers continually work on new designs and ideas to capture and make use of animal waste.

Biogas is perhaps the ultimate energy source, allowing farmers to produce their own electricity and reduce the water contamination, odor pollution, and global warming emissions caused by animal waste.

Anaerobic Digester Process

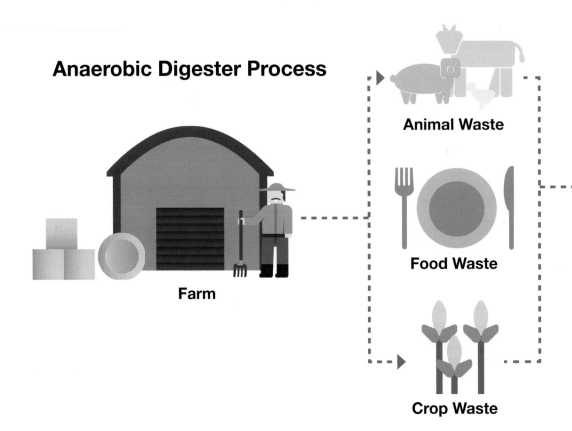

Farm

Animal Waste

Food Waste

Crop Waste

The AgSTAR program was set up by the United States Environmental Protection Agency (EPA) to promote the use of recovery systems that produce biogas. More than a hundred livestock farms in the U.S. are taking part in the program. They use anaerobic digesters designed for livestock farms, many of which the farmers invent or adapt to their specific needs. The systems help produce electricity to run the farm, often making them total self-sustaining operations. In 2014, farming biogas systems were providing enough **renewable** energy to power about 20,000 homes. In the U.S. there are more than 240 digester systems in use at commercial livestock farms. Most of them are using the biogas produced to generate electricity. But some are also further processing the biogas to produce fuel for transportation.

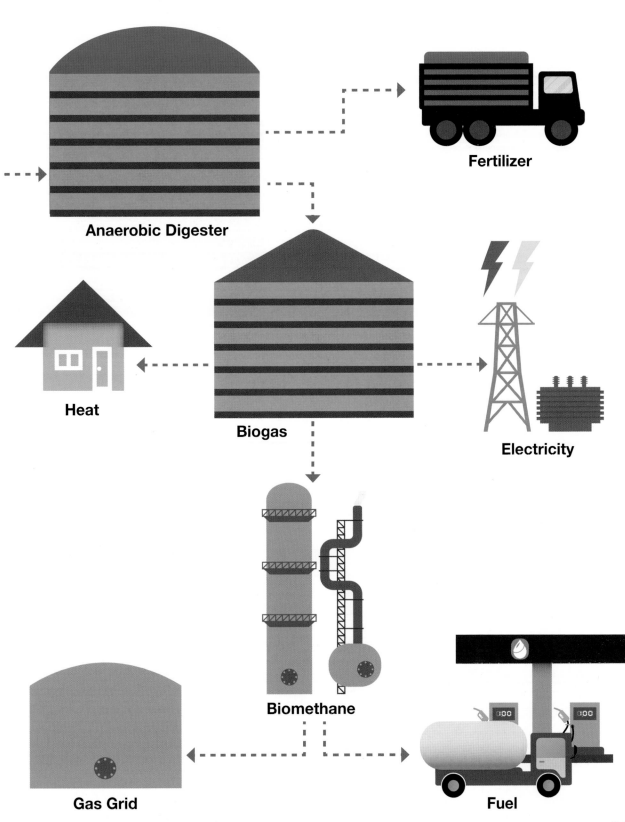

Anaerobic Digester

Fertilizer

Heat

Biogas

Electricity

Biomethane

Gas Grid

Fuel

Pig manure offers a bigger challenge to farmers. Their manure is not only one of the smelliest, it contaminates groundwater and releases more harmful gases in addition to methane, such as hydrogen sulfide and ammonia. And farmers raise a lot of pigs—billions of them, in fact.

Scientists from the University of Illinois figured out a method to convert pig poop into crude oil. They imitated the process that created oil from dinosaur bones and other ancient organic material, but they sped up the process in their lab by using a metal reactor. The oil they produced could potentially be used as a replacement for the crude oil we extract from the Earth!

Poop Lagoons

Most large-scale pig farmers have a method called the lagoon-and-spray-field system to handle the millions of tons of manure produced by their pigs annually. They flush all the pig waste into open-air pits. Then they spray that liquid poop on the surrounding fields to keep the lagoons from overflowing. Researchers are figuring out ways to get energy from these lagoons and help reduce the negative impacts they can have on the environment.

Many zoos around the world compost animal waste to create fertilizer. The Denver Zoo in Colorado is working to build a large gasification plant on its premises. The goal is to turn 90 percent of its animal and human waste into power to heat water and buildings at the facility. They even have a "Poop to Power Science Lab" where students can design, build, and test mini-versions of a **gasifier** that produces a product called syngas. In 2011, the zoo's "Waste to Energy" goals along with its sustainable features earned it the first "Greenest Zoo" award from the Association of Zoos and Aquariums.

Gasification is a process that heats organic waste at a high temperature in a low oxygen environment, creating syngas, which is a combination of carbon monoxide, carbon dioxide, and hydrogen gas. Anaerobic digestion is a process that composts organic waste products into biogas, which is a combination of methane and carbon dioxide.

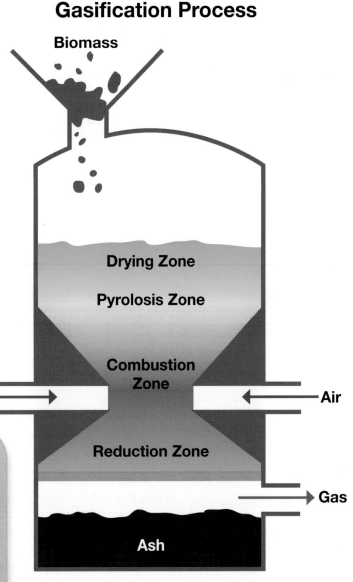

Gasification Process

Biomass

Drying Zone

Pyrolosis Zone

Combustion Zone

Air

Reduction Zone

Gas

Ash

A zoo in France has taken advantage of one of its abundant resources—animal poop—to use in technology that converts waste to electricity by burning biogas. Two pandas will contribute 65 pounds of fuel to the effort every day. The technology will help the zoo cut electricity costs by about 40 percent.

Some poop is more powerful than other poop. For instance, pandas have unique microbes in their waste because they only eat pretty much one thing: bamboo. If you've ever munched on a bamboo stick, you probably know that it would not be very easy to digest.

Scientists at the Mississippi State University discovered that pandas have super-digesting microbes in their digestion process that work to break down the bamboo. The same microbes could break down by-products that can be used to make biofuel. If the scientists can figure out how to grow the microbes on a massive scale, they could harvest them for biofuel production.

What does that mean? Currently, a lot of biofuel is made from corn, which is also a major food source for the world. Some people disagree with using it for power. While the by-products of corn such as the husks and cobs could be used to create biofuel, the process of breaking down the tough fiber and plant matter is a costly extra step. A natural solution such as panda super-microbes might be just the ticket to help bolster the biofuel industry and make people less reliant on fossil fuel. And it's also a win for pandas, which are an endangered species.

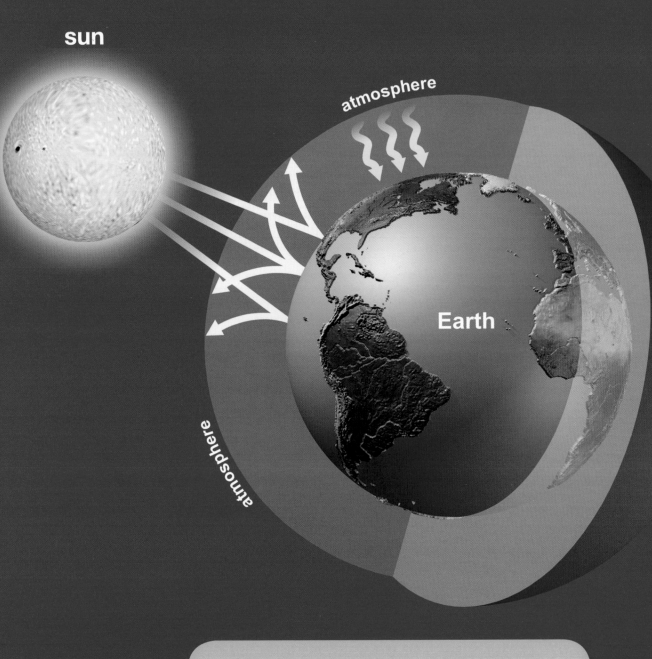

The second most common greenhouse gas produced in the U.S. from human activities is methane (CH4). Even though carbon dioxide (CO_2) is more prevalent, because methane is much more effective at trapping heat than carbon dioxide, the impact of methane on climate change is thought to be 25 times greater than carbon dioxide.

BUILDING A BETTER POOP DIGESTER

The process of converting poop into energy using a digester can be a fairly simple process. A good example is the design created by Leroy Mwasaru and his classmates. While more large-scale systems are being used on big livestock farm operations in the U.S. and other countries, efficient and inexpensive ways to create biogas can be tricky in places where energy is most needed and money and resources are most scarce. It's a worldwide challenge to come up with new and improved ways to turn waste into energy!

Anaerobic Digestions Stages

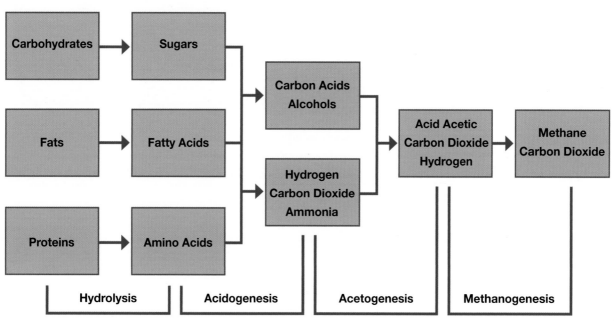

There are three commonly used digesters employed in developing countries. All three are wet digestion systems that operate continuously. This kind of system generally works better for household and small communities. There are other systems that use dry waste and/or are batch fed. Batch fed means that they are filled up, closed, and left for a period of time. Then they are opened, emptied, and refilled.

Fixed dome digesters are one of the most well-known biogas generators in the world. These simple, typically underground generators originated in China sometime around 1936. Due to their relative simplicity and use of readily available materials both as fuel and in construction, fixed dome digesters have become increasingly popular throughout the world.

One of the three common designs is a fixed-dome digester. It is usually built out of clay bricks on a circular concrete base. The sides taper in, much like an igloo.

Fixed-Dome Digester

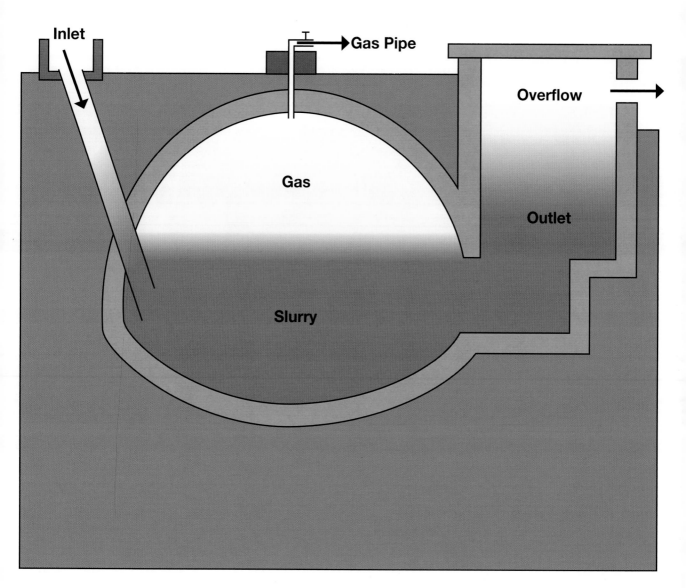

When completed, the digester is back-filled with soil. Livestock waste is put into the mixing unit along with urine and available water. Gravity causes the mixed sludge to go to the bottom of the unit.

140 cows produce about 5,600 tons (5,080 metric tons) of manure a year. That poop can potentially produce about 270,000 kWh (kilowatt hours) of energy. That's about 950 kWh per day, enough energy to power 30 average U.S. homes. Considering there were about 90 million cows in the U.S. in 2015, there is a lot of energy potential in cow poop!

As anaerobic processes get to work, biogas is produced and stored inside the digester. As the gas slowly builds up, it pushes the digested mud into an expansion chamber. Some of it then moves back to be digested more, and the rest travels into a holding tank where it can be stored and later used as compost or fertilizer. The dome digester has no moving parts, so it doesn't cost much to maintain, and it is fairly easy to use.

Another digester design is called a floating drum digester. In a simple version, a movable drum floats in the digesting slurry that resides in another drum. A mixture of waste and water is poured into an inlet pipe where it travels to the bottom of the digester. Gas is stored in the floating tank. The tank rises and falls depending on how much gas it has collected inside of it.

Agricultural small scale anaerobic digesters, like the fixed-dome or floating-drum, can help to cover distributed energy demands.

Floating Drum Digester

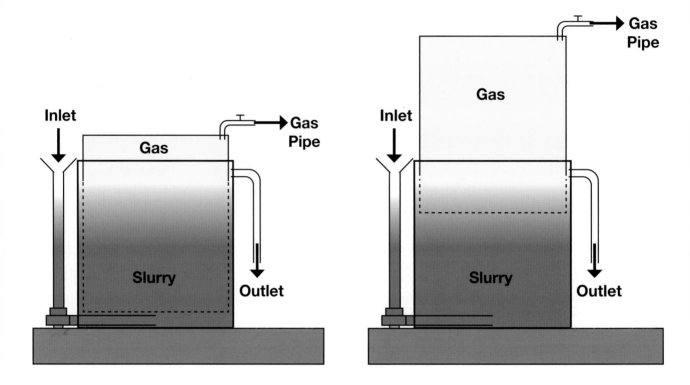

This simple system isn't as dependable or maintenance-free as a dome digester, but is popular for household use because it is simple and fairly inexpensive to make if the drums are available. Larger floating drum digesters usually have the digester underground with the floating tank on the surface.

A tubular digester is the other commonly used system. Also called a balloon digester, the system uses a plastic or rubber bag as a digester and a gas collector all in one. The balloon is tubular, with the inlet at

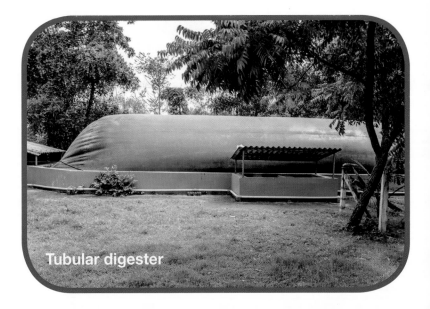

Tubular digester

one end and the outlet on the other. It is installed so that most of it is underground, with the gas pipe coming out the top. A tubular digester is also a fairly inexpensive system, but it can be fragile and easily damaged by animals or sunlight. It usually lasts only a few years.

Tubular Digester

Gas Pipe

Inlet

Gas

Outlet

Slurry

All anaerobic digesters use a natural process to break down organic matter. Containing the methane gas until it is burned has a lot of environmental benefits. These systems also help to reduce odors from sewage and cut back on the amount of harmful **pathogens** that are present in decaying waste. People can improve their waste disposal systems, reduce greenhouse gas emissions and deforestation, and generate inexpensive cooking fuel that could decrease or even replace the use of wood, propane, and charcoal.

Schools, hospitals, prisons, government buildings, and tourist accommodations can all benefit from the biogas produced by these innovative poop digesters.

Mooooo ... Burp!

Cows and other animals let loose a lot of methane by burping. In the U.S., cow belching is believed to account for more than a quarter of methane emissions. One method of capturing it involves a special harness and a gas tank tied to the cow. But scientists think they have a more efficient way of dealing with all that gas. They added a compound to the cow's food that stopped a lot of the burping.

AirCarbon — a thermoplastic that can be shaped into many things and has the performance properties of petroleum-based plastic has been made into hard, durable casings, as well as thin films and bulky furniture.

Poop to Plastic?

Several companies are working to use biogas to make plastics. One company, called Newlight, converts gas from a dairy farm close to their facility into a material they call AirCarbon. They sell AirCarbon to companies that manufacture finished plastic products. Competition is fierce because plastics are usually made from oil or natural gas, but this idea is another way people can deal with environmental issues caused by the use of fossil fuels and make use of our huge supply of methane gas.

Activity

It's a Gas!

You can demonstrate how biogas is produced using only a plastic bottle, a balloon, and a few bits of organic material (no poop needed!):

You will need:
- large plastic beverage bottle
- party balloon
- one tablespoon (15 milliliters) raw ground beef
- two lettuce leaves, torn into small pieces
- two tablespoons (30 milliliters) sand
- two teaspoons (10 milliliters) water
- eight inches (20.32 centimeters) of string or strong rubber band
- masking tape or other strong tape

What you do:
- This is best as a demonstration for smaller children. It is important to wash hands after handling the raw meat.
- Place the meat and lettuce bits into the plastic bottle.
- Wash hands!
- Pour the sand so that it covers the meat and lettuce. Do not shake the bottle to mix.
- Slowly add the water so that it trickles down the sides of the bottle, not directly on the sand.
- Stretch the neck of the balloon over the mouth of the bottle.
- Tie the balloon with the string or rubber band and wrap it with masking tape.
- Place the bottle in a warm place and observe for the next three days.

Results: The organic material begins to decay and the balloon inflates because of the biogas that was produced. Be sure to discard everything in a plastic bag and dispose of properly.

$E_k = \frac{1}{2}mv^2$

energy
object
of an ob
of an ob

When testing your experiment in a lab, it is important to wear proper safety equipment and always have adult supervision from a teacher or parent.

PROS AND CONS OF POOP POWER

Many of the positive reasons to use power from poop have already been pointed out. There is the abundant supply and it's renewable, so we'll always have plenty of it in the future. Producing power from our garbage and sewage is a good way to deal with the billions of tons of waste that humans create and dispose of, often improperly.

Charge Your Smartphone with Poop?

In late 2014, researchers from the University of East Anglia in the U.K. made great strides in learning how we might use bacteria for clean energy. As the researchers study how electrons hop using proteins from bacteria, they hope that this newly discovered natural process can be used as a form of bioenergy. Bio-batteries, which are batteries powered by organic compounds, could get their power from animal or human waste. They could then be used to power portable devices such as smartphones, laptop computers, and tablets.

Most agree that burning the methane and turning it into CO_2 and water is not as bad as allowing it to escape into the atmosphere. Making use of the methane as it burns is an even better idea. Plus, the valuable nutrients created during the process are an extra bonus.

Some farmers in the U.S. and elsewhere in the world have become completely energy independent thanks to recycling the farm's manure and crop wastes, turning it into biogas for their operations. Many farms produce enough to share with neighbors, and/or sell to local power companies and fuel suppliers. In many areas, there are incentives that encourage people to install biogas plants. Biogas is also proving to be one answer to getting power into areas that otherwise have to rely on fossil fuels. It can be a low-cost process, even something a family or community can build using recycled or repurposed materials.

Alternative, renewable energy sources can also help curtail climate change. Climate change is the term used to describe changes in the weather patterns on Earth. There are many factors that can contribute to climate change, some of them naturally occurring, such as volcanic activity. But most scientists link climate change to human activities, especially our large-scale use of fossil fuels and the waste produced by our gigantic livestock industry.

Biogas by its nature lessens the emissions that contribute to climate change. The CO_2 released when burning biogas is nearly matched by the organic materials that were used to create it. Plants use CO_2 from the atmosphere in order to grow. This would include the grasses and grains fed to cattle and other livestock, and all those vegetables, grains and fruit your parents made you eat. This means that unlike fossil fuels, biogas is pretty much **carbon-neutral**.

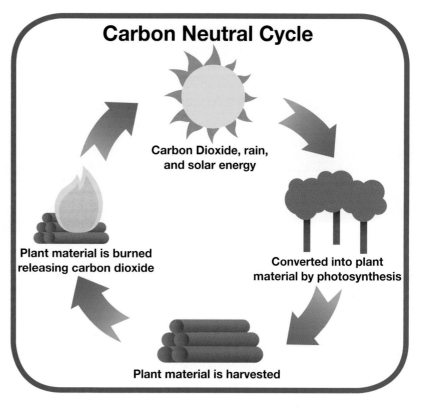

Carbon Neutral Cycle

Carbon Dioxide, rain, and solar energy

Converted into plant material by photosynthesis

Plant material is harvested

Plant material is burned releasing carbon dioxide

In 2014, U.S. President Barack Obama introduced *the Biogas Opportunities Roadmap*. Research proved that the biogas industry had great potential, but there were too few biogas systems in use. Thousands of livestock operations could produce and use or sell biogas. If enough farms got involved, enough energy could be produced to power a million average U.S. homes! The plan encourages voluntary expansion of the biogas industry and works with investors to develop new technologies. About 8,000 more farms have the opportunity to reduce greenhouse gas emissions and benefit by the advancement of biogas energy technology.

Although biogas plants are still a controversial subject, they may be the most likely way to convert the power we need while using readily available materials and saving the planet all at the same time.

Still, biogas is not a perfect renewable energy resource. The processes often require water, and although water can often be recaptured, in areas where it is precious or unavailable, many systems can't be used. Harvesting the biogas from landfills means that toxic waste that could be present must be addressed, causing additional processes and expense. Installing operational anaerobic digesters into the places most in need requires money, materials, and skilled labor, 44 which are often not easy to come by.

Still, many people agree that, of all the materials that can be used to create biomass energy, poop makes the most sense. Some even call it an "attractive" source of alternative energy. Imagine that.

A Human Poop-Powered City Bus!

In 2014, the Bath Bus Company in the United Kingdom partnered with GENeco, the city of Bristol's sewage treatment system operators, to power a city bus with human waste. Called the Bio-Bus, this poop-powered vehicle can go a long way, and it gets a lot of positive attention from the public. Officials told reporters they would run it on the "number two route ... because that seems to sort of ring a bell with people."

GLOSSARY

anaerobic (AE-nuh-RO-bik): able to live or act without any oxygen

bioenergy (bye-oh-en-ur-jee): renewable energy made from biological sources

biogas (BYE-oh-gass): gases produced by the breakdown of organic materials in the absence of oxygen

biomass (BYE-oh-mass): the name given to living or recently living things that are a potential source of energy

bioreactor (bye-oh-ree-AK-tur): a vessel used to grow organisms

carbon-neutral (KAR-buhn NOO-truhl): relating to a process or activity that matches or surpasses the amount of carbon released by the amount of carbon it removed from the environment

gasifier (GASS-uh-fire): a machine that produces gas

methane (METH-ane): a colorless gas that burns easily

microorganisms (MYE-kroh-OR-guh-niz-uhmz): living things that can't be seen without a microscope

nitrates (NYE-trates): the salts of nitric acid

pathogens (PATH-uh-juhns): agents that can cause disease

prototype (PROH-tuh-tipe): the first version of an invention that tries out an idea to see if it works

renewable (ri-NOO-uh-buhl): something that replenishes and can't be used up

sustainable (suh-STAYN-uh-buhl): able to be maintained at a certain rate or level

INDEX

anaerobic   10, 12, 21-23, 25, 29, 33, 36, 44, 46

Bio-Bus   45

bioenergy   8, 19, 40

biogas   5-7, 9, 10, 12, 19, 21-23, 25, 29, 33, 36-38, 41, 43, 44, 46

compost   5, 9, 10, 21, 25, 33

energy   9-11, 14-16, 22, 24, 25, 29, 32, 40-47

Environmental Protection Agency   22

farms   22, 29, 37, 41, 43

methane   5, 7, 10, 21, 24, 25, 28, 29, 36, 37, 41, 46

resources   4, 11, 14, 29

sanitation   6, 13, 14

sewage   4, 5, 21, 36, 40, 45

sustainable   14, 25, 46

toilet(s)   10, 11, 12-17, 19-21

SHOW WHAT YOU KNOW

1. What kinds of uses does dried dung have? Why is it a good idea to wash your hands after handling it?
2. What kinds of bioenergy systems can you name and explain?
3. What is anaerobic digestion? What is it good for?
4. What are the advantages of using poop power compared with other sources of energy?
5. Based on what you've read about the power of poop, why do you think people would rather rely on fossil fuels than on alternative forms of energy such as biomass energy?

WEBSITES TO VISIT

http://ei.lehigh.edu/eli/energy/resources/readings/biomass.pdf

http://epa.gov/climatestudents/solutions/technologies/methane.html

www.education.com/science-fair/environmental-issues

ABOUT THE AUTHOR

Robin Koontz is a freelance author/illustrator/ designer of a wide variety of nonfiction and fiction books, educational blogs, and magazine articles for children and young adults. Her 2011 science title, *Leaps and Creeps – How Animals Move to Survive,* was an Animal Behavior Society Outstanding Children's Book Award finalist. Raised in Maryland and Alabama, Robin now lives with her husband in the Coast Range of western Oregon where she especially enjoys observing the wildlife on her property. You can learn more on her blog: robinkoontz.wordpress.com

Meet The Author!
www.meetREMauthors.com

© 2016 Rourke Educational Media

All rights reserved. No part of this book may be reproduced or utilized in any form or by any means, electronic or mechanical including photocopying, recording, or by any information storage and retrieval system without permission in writing from the publisher.

www.rourkeeducationalmedia.com

PHOTO CREDITS: Cover © Elenaphoto21, Kateryna Kon, EtiAmmos, Loskutnikov; Page 4 © tzahiV; Page 5 © Santosh Varghese; Page 6 © sciencepics; Page 7 © RussieseO, ToddSm66; Page 8 © Pixelfusion3d; Page 9 © rvimages; Page 10 © Zavalynuk Sergey; Page 12 © Michael Utech; Page 13 © lembi; Page 14 © Associated Press - Ted S. Warren; Page 17, 18 © NASA; Page 18 © NASA - Bill Stafford ; Page 19 © Prasit Rodphan, Acerebel; Page 20 © jrleyland; Page 21 © Ulrich Mueller; Page 24 © Juriaan Huting, Timrobertsaerial; Page 26 © uschools, Oktay Orakcioglu; Page 27 © Bill Oxford; Page 28 © Vitoriano Junior; Page 30 © Wysiati; Page 32 © R Carner; Page 33 © ADISAK SOIFA; Page 35 © Sukkunta Suppajit; Page 36 © remco86; Page 37 © makanis, poplasen; Page 39 © Pamela Moore; Page 40 © ponsulak; Page 41 © Karl-Friedrich Hohl; Page 42 © Gadaian; Page 43 © CreativeNature_nl; Page 44 © FRANK HOFFMANN; Page 45 © AP - Simon Chapman/LNP Rex

Special Thanks to RTI International www.rti.org, www.abettertoilet.org

Edited by: Keli Sipperley

Cover and Interior design by: Nicola Stratford   www.nicolastratford.com

Library of Congress PCN Data

Poop is Power! / Robin Koontz
(Let's Explore Science)
ISBN 978-1-68191-389-6 (hard cover)
ISBN 978-1-68191-431-2 (soft cover)
ISBN 978-1-68191-470-1 (e-Book)
Library of Congress Control Number: 2015951556

Also Available as:

Printed in the United States of America, North Mankato, Minnesota